The Publishers deny all knowledge of any assistance provided by Agent Pavel Ivanisovitch, Agent Igor Rostropovich, Cmdr Nicolas Alexandrov, Agent Maxim Ovseyenko, Dr Alexei Modestov, Agent Georg Chuyev, Director Anatoly Frolov and the Senior Councils of the S.V.R. and the F.S.B. in the preparation of this book, and would like to extend their heartfelt and secret spasibos for the lack of assistance received.

Publishers: Ladybird Books Ltd., Loughborough
Printed in England. If wet, Italy.

A Ladybird book about
DONALD TRUMP

by J.A. HAZELEY, N.S.F.W.
and J.P. MORRIS, O.M.G.

(Authors of 'Scrooge McDuck: The Art of The Deal')

A LADYBIRD BOOK FOR GROWN-UPS

The United States of America is the most powerful country in the world, and its President is the most powerful person in the world.

Anyone can grow up to become President.

Or they can become President first, and think about growing up later.

Donald has very big hands.

The best hands.

Donald measures his hands. They are still very, very big. And getting bigger every day.

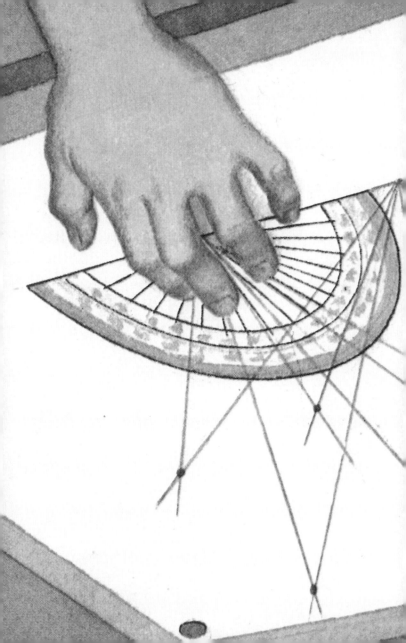

Donald has called an important meeting.

It is with all his closest work colleagues who are not in prison.

Here they both are.

Donald likes gas and oil.

Gas and oil are the very best ways of making power.

Relying on gas and oil means nobody needs to live near the noise of a sustainable windmill, which might give them cancer.

The failing newspapers do not report how good Donald is because they are jealous.

They are not the President. A newspaper has never been the President. A paper President would just blow away in the wind.

Donald is not frightened of the wind. But he does sometimes wear a baseball cap in case the wind wants to play with his new hair.

Nelbert works in the factory where Donald's hair is made.

He earns three dollars an hour bonding biphenyl polyethylovinyl strands to a polythene tri—weave cranial mat which attaches to the existing hair using an acrylic adhesive.

Nelbert has chemical lung damage — but it is worth it to achieve such a natural look.

Executive Time is the important half of the day when Donald watches television to find some opinions he can have.

Donald tweets, "Failing elephants are SAD. If crazy weird trunk guys threaten USA they will face CONSEQUENCES LIKE NEVER BE SEEN! Crooked Dumbos."

Donald thinks he is watching Fox News, but he has turned on National Geographic by mistake.

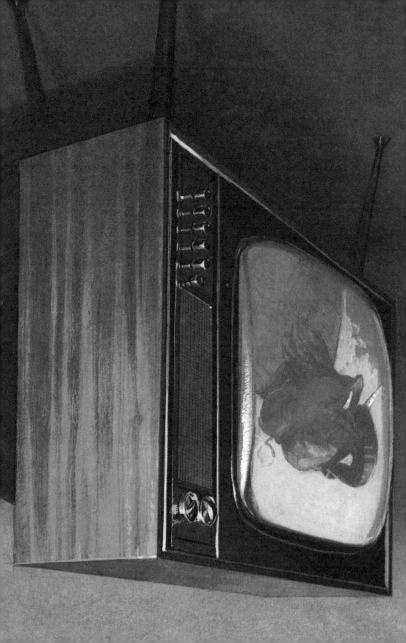

Like anyone with good taste, Donald likes things that are completely covered in gold.

This is his new chest freezer. It is full of hamburgers.

The hamburgers are not covered in gold, but when someone finds a way of doing that, those will be the hamburgers Donald buys.

Donald likes the cat.

Donald likes to touch the cat.

But Donald accidentally tells a television presenter he likes to touch the cat.

Now Donald is in trouble.

Donald does not understand.

Donald has commissioned a painting of himself, exactly as he looks now, winning a prize for jumping over a candle–stick.

"Many people say I am the best at jumping over candle–sticks," says Donald, and in the painting that is very true.

In real life, Donald cannot jump over candle–sticks, because of bone spurs.

These men are building Donald's new tower in Soligorsk.

To build his tower, Donald needed help from his Russian best friends.

The interesting thing about Donald's Russian best friends is that he does not have any Russian best friends and they do not exist and this page is a witch hunt.

Like many golfers, Donald has his own set of clubs. This one is Mar–a–Lago, in Florida.

Donald does not ever cheat at golf. Cheating makes winning too easy.

Except in the election where it was the loser Crooked Hillary who did all the cheating.

Silly Hillary. She might as well not have cheated at all.

Some people think that Donald's wife is sometimes not Donald's wife but someone pretending to be Donald's wife.

That cannot be true, because Donald's wife can be easily recognised by her very large sunglasses and the long hair covering her face.

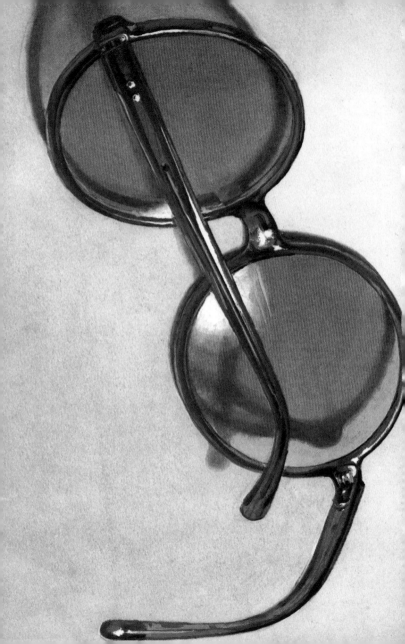

Donald likes to make terrible things nearly happen, and then stop them at the last minute.

That way he can say he stopped a terrible thing from happening.

It is a shame he forgot to do this when he was still only nearly President.

Donald's wife is visited by the ghost of Donald's mother.

"I'm sorry," says Donald's mother. "I didn't know that ignoring him as a child would make him into such an unbearable adult."

"Why did you ignore him?" asks Donald's wife.

"Because he was such an unbearable child," says Donald's mother.

When Donald is asked to think about hard questions he says, "We'll see." And sometimes he says, "You'll see."

What will happen next? Donald does not know.

But it will be seen.

He was right about that.

Donald has an imaginary friend called Covfefe.

Covfefe does not lie about Donald or witch—hunt him or say he is not the best.

If only real people could be more like Covfefe.

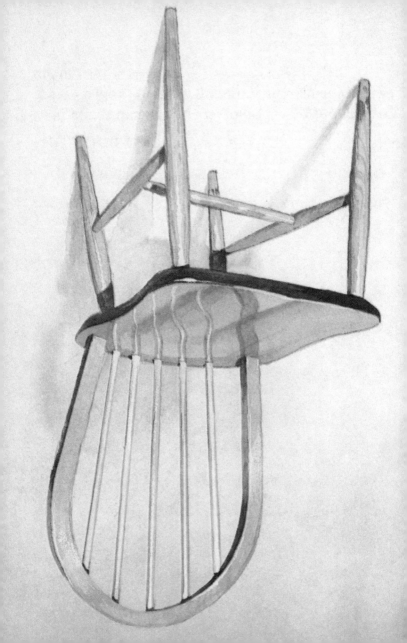

Some racists have had a big fight with some not—racists.

"There were very fine people on both sides," says Donald.

The not—racists are shocked. But Donald said a nice thing. He said they were as good as the racists.

Donald just wants to make everybody as happy as he makes the racists.

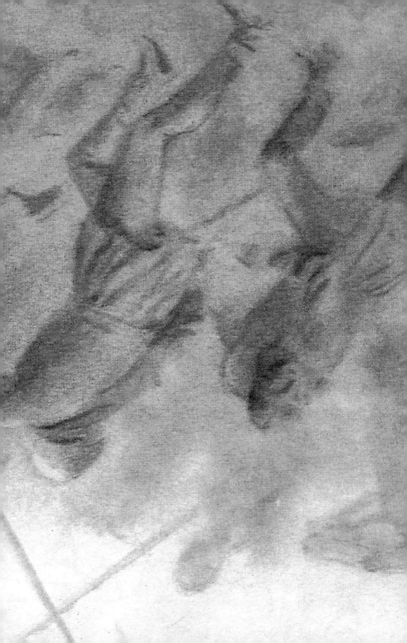

Before he was President, Donald's job was being a millionaire. He had been doing this job since he was eight years old.

Donald made his millions by taking them from his father, and then trying not to lose as many of them as he could.

If everyone was as clever as Donald, everyone could be a millionaire.

Donald knows guns are a good way to deal with bad people.

If bad people use guns too, everything can be fixed using thoughts and prayers.

If bad people ever learned to use thoughts and prayers, who knows what bad things might happen.

Luckily the bad people only have guns.

Donald's speech—writers have learned to write speeches so they sound just like Donald talking.

But Donald does not like learning the speeches. Reading is hard.

Donald likes to think of the words out of his own head instead.

Donald has the best words.

Peter, have a sweet.
Have some sweets.
Have some sweets, Peter.

America is great again.

Donald has built a wall, so only Americans can enjoy how great again America is.

Old black and white photographs where Americans appear to have come into America from other countries are fake news.

"People are saying I'm the best President ever," says Donald.

"People are saying I'm very, very intelligent," says Donald.

"People are saying my approval ratings are the highest ever," says Donald.

All these People are Donald.

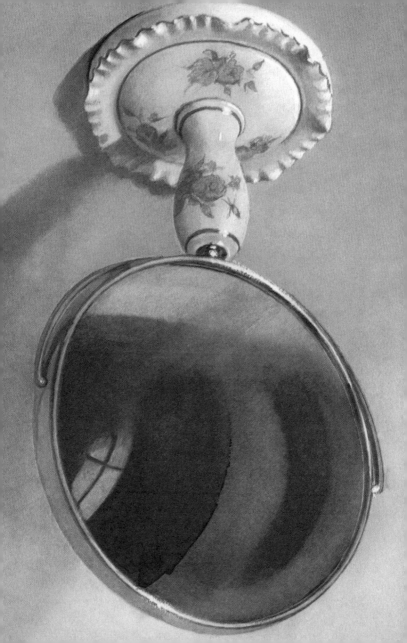

When Donald won the election, he did not believe it.

"This election was a bad, unfair election," said Donald, about the election that he won.

One day, Donald might lose an election. He will not like that election at all.

And when Donald is told it is time to stop being the President, who knows what exciting things will happen next?

THE AUTHORS would like to record their gratitude and offer their apologies to the many Ladybird artists whose luminous work formed the glorious wallpaper of countless childhoods. Revisiting it for this book as grown-ups has been a privilege.

MICHAEL JOSEPH

UK | USA | Canada | Ireland | Australia
India | New Zealand | South Africa

Michael Joseph is part of the Penguin Random House group of companies
whose addresses can be found at global.penguinrandomhouse.com
First published 2019
001

Printed in Italy by L.E.G.O. S.p.A

A CIP catalogue record for this book is available from the British Library

ISBN: 978–0–241–42272–4

www.greenpenguin.co.uk

MIX
Paper from
responsible sources
FSC® C018179

Penguin Random House is committed to a
sustainable future for our business, our readers
and our planet. This book is made from Forest
Stewardship Council® certified paper.